It's the Thought That Counts...

For Better or For Worse
Fifteenth Anniversary Collection

by Lynn Johnston

Andrews and McMeel
A Universal Press Syndicate Company
Kansas City

Library of Congress Catalog Card Number: 94-71738

ISBN: 0-8362-1762-4

For my family and
friends who contribute
in so many ways
to the stories in
For Better or
For Worse

Introduction

It was a hot and sultry night. Jim Davis (creator of Garfield), Mike Peters (creator of Mother Goose and Grimm), and I sat at a banquet table, invitees to a benefit dinner for the Sarasota Hospital. We were well into our second bottle of wine, when a Garfield fan sat down next to Jim and said, "Mr. Davis, I've always wondered; where *do* you get your ideas!?" Without missing a beat, Jim replied, "Schenectady." Satisfied, the inquiring mind wandered off. "That must be the question we're most often asked," I ruminated. Mike voted for: How far ahead of the deadline do you have to be? and Jim agreed.

In fact, he had considered having a T-shirt made with "six weeks, dailies" on the front and "eight weeks, Sundays" on the back. Then, when someone posed the chestnut opener, he would simply open his jacket and expose the appropriate response. This, of course, led to the proposal that we design the "benefit suit," imprinted everywhere with answers to all the questions a syndicated cartoonist is asked most often.

Oddly enough, the questions our readers most often ask us are the questions we ask each other and the toughest ones to answer. The toughest question has always been, "How do you get your ideas?"

How do you answer that? It's like asking runners how they run, or singers how they sing. They just do it!

We are all born with wonderful gifts. We use these gifts to express ourselves, to amuse, to strengthen, and to communicate. We begin as children to explore and develop our talents, often unaware that we are unique, that not everyone can do what we're doing!

I loved to draw funny pictures. If they got me into trouble, it was worth it. If they made people laugh, I was high. By the time I was in my teens, I knew I would be a cartoonist. I never imagined, however, that I would, someday, have the great fortune (and awesome responsibility) of producing a comic feature that would be read daily by millions of people worldwide.

Jim and Mike and I—and all of the people I know in this business—have all been overwhelmed by this "work" we do. We have heard Charles Schulz say, "Can you believe we really do this for a living?" Looking back on forty-five years of drawing Peanuts, he has said on several occasions, "How do we think of all of those things, anyway?!!!"

Where do the ideas come from?

For most of us, drawing comes easily—but, without ideas, there are no drawings! Truly, in this business, it's the thought that counts!

You begin with a blank page. When you have a deadline, a blank page is both a threat and a challenge! How do you create something from nothing? Somehow, we do it—and we love what we do.

Our methods vary. Some of us doodle, some of us sit, some of us work with writers. All of us know that the process can be difficult and we have to prepare in advance for those times when, no matter how hard we try, nothing comes, nothing works . . . and the blank page scores against us.

Because I still consider it something of a riddle, I wanted to try and describe what happens during those creative times when the writing is done—at least how it's done for For Better or For Worse.

On a lazy Saturday morning when you're lying in bed, drifting in and out of sleep, there is a space where fantasy and reality become one. Are you awake, or are you dreaming? You see people and things, some are familiar, some are strange. You talk, you feel, but you move without walking; you fly without wings. Your mind and your body exist, but on separate planes. Time stands still. For me, this is the feeling I have when ideas come.

There is a small sun room off our bedroom that overlooks a thick stand of birch trees. In this room, I keep a beach chair, an old carved table, some plants, a telephone, and a large wooden flamingo. This is my "writing place." It is here that I go to await inspiration! I wait and I wait and . . . I wait.

Like starting an old chainsaw that's hard to start, you often have to apply every trick of the trade before work can begin! One idea-generator is the matching together of random things, let's say: a sock, a banana, and a typewriter, for example. I can then see April, one sock off, one sock on, kneeling on a chair, mashing a banana into her mother's typewriter. Aha—a daily!

If this doesn't work, I pace the floor, I go through material I have just sent in . . . I think about the characters and whose turn it is to be heard from next. I flick through the channels of my imagination, hoping to find something good, something I can build on, something funny!

Sometimes, there are voices without pictures. Sometimes there are pictures without words. I observe my cartoon family by hovering above them like a visiting spirit.

Sometimes I become the characters themselves. I think their thoughts and feel what they feel. Always, I wait for things to happen. I wait for them to speak, to be spoken to.

I cannot always predict what the characters will say or how their world will evolve around them. I am often surprised by their conversations. There are times when they seem to take charge; take the stories where they want them to go!

Still, the director's chair is mine, and when a clash of wills happens and the writing stops . . . it's time to get up, get out, and break away from it all. (I usually raid the fridge, which is one of the hazards of working at home.)

Each cast member in For Better or For Worse is based on someone I know well. Elizabeth, for example, responds to situations the way my daughter Katie might respond. Her school is Kate's school, her body language and speech patterns are similar. Elizabeth Patterson, however, is also *me*. She has my childhood memories, my private thoughts, my passions, goals, and fears. She is me, she is my daughter, she is an imaginary girl of thirteen who has, believe it or not . . . a very definite mind of her own.

I am every character (even the dog) and, yet, every character is an entity unto itself. This concept, although complex and confusing to others, is part of the routine. No wonder cartoonists need an understanding family! Our minds are always "somewhere else"!!

A cartoonist is a writer, an actor, a director, and an artist. We write, act, and direct every scene. Even the camera work is important! The drawing is the final stage of the production and the time, for me, when I can touch these imaginary images, feel them, bring them to life!

Penciling my thoughts first, frame by frame, expression by expression, I act out every movement. I picture every scene and project that image onto the page—in pencil. When the panels are completed, the inking is done. Inking the drawings is an experience I always look forward to. It's like having a ghost in front of me, and by reaching out, moving my pen around its form, touching it, pressing against its face, its body, feeling it, I make it real. This part of my job is pure pleasure! After all these years, I still think of it as a kind of "magic," and I wonder how and why this magic was entrusted to me!

Knowing the other people in this industry with whom I share so much has been one of my greatest joys. We are what we do. I have admired some of these people for years. Some are contemporaries, some just coming through the door! All are open and giving. All of us reveal more of ourselves in the work that we do than our readers will ever know.

These small hand-drawn characters are projections of ourselves. The part that none of us can ever quite explain, however, is the wit and the wisdom. Where does it come from? The sarcasm, the laughter, the wry turn of the phrase! Do we tap into a mental reservoir? Is there a spiritual connection to cartoonists from the past who'll say "Psst—try this one!!!" If so—where are they when we need them the most?

I do know that a great deal of material does come from home. It comes from family and friends, from the present, the past . . . from something said, just in passing. I have done many drawings for For Better or For Worse that came from real experiences. I thought it might be of interest, perhaps, if I took some of these and explained how and why I did them.

Here, then, is a selection of Sunday pages that are sort of a glimpse into our family album. I hope these private snapshots help to shed some light on where the ideas come from . . . because . . . to tell you the truth . . . I still don't really know!

This is my fifteenth anniversary collection. I hope you enjoy it.

Sincerely,

When our daughter, Katie, was fourteen, I took her to New York City for a holiday. It was going to be one of those great parent-child "togetherness" times when we would bond in mutual respect and understanding.

Unfortunately, this effort fails should the parent make any noticeable gestures that draw attention to the fact that he or she exists.

When I tripped and rolled down the great carpeted stairway in one of the theaters, Kate thought she was going to die. Her look of horror was a look I well remember. I have been on the other side of that look many times.

We often accompanied our parents to their favorite restaurant, the Ho Inn, and it was a tradition that my brother and I should suffer supreme humiliation as Dad read aloud the menu . . . in Chinese. The waiters knew him well, encouraged him by correcting his pronunciation, and enjoyed the effect this subtle torture had on Alan and me, who sat there wishing for all the world that we were somewhere else.

No matter what the circumstances, teenagers do not wish to be seen with or near their parents. Unless food or money or shelter or the comforting shoulder of authority are needed, parents are uncool and to be avoided if at all possible.

As we waited for our order, I sat, glaring at my place mat, listening to my parents chatter. They talked too loud. They laughed too much. I decided to kill time by going to the bathroom. Head lowered in my customary posture *de* petulance, I swung out of my chair and stood up. Our waiter didn't have time to get out of my way and I hit his large metal tray with the side of my head. Corn soup and other stuff sprayed everywhere. Time stopped. Everything stopped. And everyone looked at me.

I still remember that to be one of my most embarrassing moments. If I really get into it, I remember my father reading the menu aloud in Chinese and I think to myself, "How could he do that to me. How could he embarrass us like that—in public?!!"

13

It rained a lot in Vancouver. As a child, I played indoors more often than out . . . sitting on the hardwood floor, melting Plasticine on the radiator.

We had sheer curtains in our dining room and twice a year they were washed. The dust that hung in the air after they were taken down was made visible by narrow beams of sunlight that filtered through our window.

The tiny particles would drift and swirl making the beams look solid, somehow. I made Plasticine shapes and stuck them on the windowsill breaking the beams to make shadows. I ran my hands along the shafts of light convinced that I could feel them. I believed that if I pretended hard enough, angels or fairies or something magical would appear.

My mother was a hard worker. She returned to the dining room with the clean curtains. She knelt down beside me, put her hand out, and said, "Where does it come from? . . . Look at all that dust!!!"

I didn't know what she was talking about. To my mind, all of it was sunshine!

I wish I still had my childhood ability to fantasize. All too often I find myself looking at something wonderful . . . but seeing only dust!

Hope, B.C., is a small town just two hours' drive inland from Vancouver. It's hidden in a valley that draws in rich, damp air from the Fraser River, turning it to mist against the mountainsides.

My parents lived there for many years, and it seemed to me that every time we visited them, it rained—just enough to make a rainbow.

In the summer of 1990, my dad, then a widower, was seriously ill with cancer. I had gone to stay with him, knowing it would be our last time together.

One day, my Aunt Mildred and I found him wandering about the small local hospital, pushing his IV pole as though it were a papal staff. In his white and blue patient garb, he had assumed the attitude of a man of the cloth and with comically pious gestures was blessing the other patients, one by one.

Taking things seriously was not in his nature. Time and again he made us laugh through our tears.

As Mildred and I left the hospital, a light rain started to fall. Sunshine still streamed through the clouds and I said to her, "Looks like another rainbow day."

It occurred to us both that laughter and tears, like sunshine and rain, often come together. Sometimes, they make a rainbow, and rainbows bring a message of hope, faith, and optimism. We knew, after all of this was over, that we'd see him again. Dad died in 1990. This drawing was done for him.

People of my generation call these "the old songs." I know the words to many of them because my father sang them so often. He would get out his guitar or his accordion and he would imagine himself to be once again in an English pub, singing to a roomful of soldiers with a pint on the piano, and a lass on his arm.

These were the songs that helped everyone endure both the war and its aftermath. They were more than music; they were from the heart.

As teenagers, however, we'd holler, "Can't you play anything new?" Now, the "new" songs to us are the "old songs" to our children, and thanks to the men and women who fought for our freedom, they are songs about less serious things.

This Sunday page was done for Remembrance Day 1990. My son was seventeen, the same age my dad was when he enlisted. I've always thought how lucky we are to be living in this day and age.

Dad always considered himself lucky.

Perhaps our generation doesn't really know what "lucky" is!!

When I turned forty, the motherhood thing happened again. We had two grown children (one away from home) and here I was daydreaming about how nice it would be to have another baby!

Once I realized that the desire to see myself balloon to impossible proportions, suffer from multiple bodily woes (including terminal sleep loss), and give up our spare room was but a figment of premenopausal madness, I did the next best thing . . . and made one up.

Going through the various stages with Elly Patterson, we relived it all. There are countless books that detail this experience so there's no need for me to describe the wonders of being "inhabited." I do want to give one bit of advice, however, to all expectant fathers: When your wife asks if you can feel the baby kicking . . . always, always say, "Yes."

Yes, I did. I married one of the most sensitive, caring men on earth. Rod Johnston actually said these words to me. This scene actually happened. The man is a treasure . . . and a master in self-defense!

36

April was "born" on April 1, 1991. What made this sequence difficult to write was that she had to appear in both the daily and Sunday comics. Since some papers carry only one or the other, I had to coordinate the event so that continuity was maintained in both. She had to be "born again," as it were!

Since she was a figment of my imagination (all the other characters are based on real family members) the plan was to have her born on April 1—thus the name "April." With April 1 being a Monday that year, I hoped that my Sunday readers would suspend their belief just a little and allow her to arrive one day early. Not so. Following the announcement that her name would be April (because she was born on April 1), I received many letters—one blatantly critical saying that if I paid more attention to my work, I would know that she was born on March 31! One helpful soul sent a calendar. So, there you have it. She is imaginary—but only to a point.

It's amazing how seriously some readers take their comics!!

We used to have a big, hairy Old English sheepdog called Farley. Unfortunately, he didn't like children, so when Aaron came along, we tossed a coin . . . and the dog lost.

We remained dogless, even though Farley appeared in the strip, but after many adventures and two moves, we bought a small black spaniel. We called him Willy. Although Willy was adopted "for the children," he is, of course, my dog. Willy does all of the things a dog does (something painfully evident when the snow melts) and he is my constant, faithful companion. He sleeps on a chair in my studio, he's underfoot in the kitchen, I trip over him in the dark on my way to the bathroom. He is my shadow, my scraps disposal, my friend.

One of his more endearing canine traits is his tendency to nudge your arm (if he can reach it).

It doesn't require a great stretch of the imagination to put a hot coffee at the end of that arm. Drawing the results is then pure pleasure!

45

My dad's mother came to live with us when I was about ten. She had waist-length silver hair, which was always secured in a tightly braided bun.

After washing it, she would stand on our back porch and brush it in the wind 'til it was dry.

For me, it was like watching Rapunzel. For just this instant, she wasn't Grandma, but a storybook heroine. Her hair was beautiful.

My mother also let her hair grow down to her waist. It was thick golden brown. Like my grandmother, she always secured it tightly against her head, and she, too, went out onto the porch to let it dry.

Ursula Ridgway was a strict disciplinarian. I guess she had to be!! So often we were at odds with one another . . . but out there, on the porch with her long hair billowing about her face, I could see the youth and the gentleness and the real spirit that was my mother.

Later, when I was in my twenties, I let my hair grow down to my waist, and when I went out onto my balcony of my apartment to let it dry, I became one with these two women who were always a little distant, yet always so much a part of me.

My mother cut her hair and kept her braid. So did I. She died in September 1989. Her hair is coiled neatly in a drawer and tied with a ribbon, next to mine.

I took the braids out the other day and I plied them together. I thought how similar the colors were and I wished with all my heart that I could see her on that porch once again.

It's so very easy to do. Baby falls asleep in the car, and you forget she's even there.

I once left Katie in the car like this, and if it had not been for an open window and the shade from a tree, she might not have survived.

To this day, I get an ache inside just thinking about it. We chaperone and protect our children and pray that they'll be kept safe from harm . . . and yet, it's often plain, simple carelessness that costs us the lives of the ones we love most.

Note: In this drawing (and one on page 48) I inadvertently drew the baby car seat the wrong way around! Readers quickly set me straight, and subsequent scenes were done correctly

For six years, we lived in the small isolated mining town of Lynn Lake, Manitoba. Rod was the local "flying dentist." I produced my strips for Universal Press, took care of the kids, and, from time to time, went crazy.

The nearest town was sixty miles away. My friend Nancy and I would sometimes drive there and back—just for donuts! Because there were no shops to speak of, no good restaurants, and no theater, we new Northerners became an inventive lot. We made our own entertainment, we created our own events, we transplanted city slickers survived, and some of us even grew to enjoy the rustic, laid-back ambience of "the bush."

One of the most enjoyable pastimes was the weekly trip to the dump. The Lynn Lake dump was no ordinary dump. It was the repository for everything from good cast-off clothing to appliances. Anything the transient population wished to leave behind as they moved out of town was left at the "Exchange," as we called it.

We furnished our basements and fixed our boats courtesy of the Exchange. We met friends there and strolled leisurely along the embankment, examining the goods as if we were in a great, primitive outdoor Wal-Mart.

It wasn't until you found yourself dressing for the occasion, that you knew it was time to get out for a while, buy a ticket to Winnipeg, and revel again in the vast indulgences of civilization!

54

I don't think I've ever known anyone who loved "being a kid again" more than my father did. He was easily coerced away from anything serious if it meant a chance to laugh, to be silly.

It was Dad who chased us down Fifth Street on roller skates, taught us to make dandelion whistles, built us our first go-cart, and told us if we flapped our arms hard enough, we could fly.

It was Dad who set fire to our big cherry tree, trying to burn out some caterpillars. He disappeared before the fire trucks arrived, and Mom later found him down at the Olympic Hotel, playing the piano in the bar.

Dad was never more himself than when he was in the company of children. I will always remember riding on his shoulders, making kites, throwing water bombs, playing marbles. It was painful for him to see my brother and me growing up; growing past the "Daddy pick me up" times. He never really understood "Daddy, go away."

Although he enjoyed and encouraged us as older children, he missed his little ones terribly.

Alan and I were in our teens when Mom opened the door one day to see two small kids from the neighborhood sheepishly looking up at her and asking, "Can Mr. Ridgway come out and play?"

For Better or For Worse

By Lynn Johnston

'BYE! - I'M LATE, THE BUS IS COMING!

OH, NO... ELIZABETH FORGOT HER LUNCH.

AND TODAY OF ALL DAYS - WHEN I HAVE A MILLION THINGS TO DO.

I'LL HAVE TO TAKE THE BABY TO ANNE'S A FEW MINUTES EARLY.

IF I RUSH, I SHOULD GET TO THE SCHOOL BEFORE THE MORNING ANNOUNCEMENTS.

I HAVE TO STOP AT THE PAPER BEFORE I GO TO THE LIBRARY... AND BOTH ARE ON THE OTHER SIDE OF TOWN! — ALL THIS TROUBLE JUST TO DELIVER A LUNCH.

STILL, IT FEELS GOOD TO KNOW HOW MUCH SHE'LL APPRECIATE IT.

DON'T FORGET PIZZA DAY • PIZZA DAY! • WOW! WICKED! AMAZING PIZZA DAY • PIZZA DAY TODAY • IT'Z... PIZZA DAY! • TODAY DON'T MISS IT! PIZZA

For Better or For Worse

By Lynn Johnston

Z

YAWNNN

YAWWNN

CRUNCH CRUNCH

MY GOODNESS, JUST LOOK AT APRIL!

GLORP

SHE'S QUITE THE LITTLE INDIVIDUAL!

YES, SHE IS.

...WE'RE TRYING TO DECIDE WHO IN THE FAMILY SHE'S MOST LIKE!!

Under great duress, Kate cleans out her closet maybe once a year. This chore should take, perhaps, one hour—tops. Instead, however, it's a major effort that lasts for up to two days. It's not so much the stalling tactics that make this such a marathon, but a rediscovery of things long forgotten.

Toys, games, books, you name it—even the occasional unchewed gumball shows up, as if for the very first time. It's a veritable bazaar of booty, easily enough to refute the line, "You never buy me anything."

There is a danger, of course, in being the supervising parent. The last time our great cleanout took place, I found myself sitting on the floor, matching up Barbie doll clothes and body parts and thinking about all the great stuff I had when I was a kid.

Wow. What I would give to be able to shovel out my own childhood closet once again!

66

I have never really enjoyed the taste of watermelon—but, I have always loved the seeds. Slippery and torpedo-shaped, they are perfectly designed for various forms of target practice. Spitting is particularly satisfying, but a good strong thumb-to-forefinger shot method is by far the best form of propulsion.

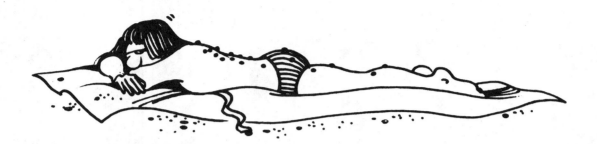

Ambleside Beach was a favorite picnic spot when we were kids. There was nothing quite like a good swim, and a big slice of sandy watermelon. With this potential ammo in hand, my brother and I would silently stalk our prey. Our favorite was the sleeping sun worshipper, hopefully face down, bikini top undone, oblivious to all but the sounds of surf and seagulls.

Watermelon seeds are painless projectiles—and, if conditions are right, you may score up to fifteen hits before your target clues in. Mega bonus points were won if our victim got up and chased us before realizing that her bikini top was still on her beach towel.

This is all from the perspective, of course, of two prepubescent youths in the sixties. Aah, those were the days! Compared to the stunts that are pulled and the flesh that is bared today . . . we were such innocents!

HMMM....I'M NOT A BAD SWIMMER FOR SOMEONE OVER 40!!

IN FACT.... I THINK I'M A BETTER SWIMMER **NOW** THAN I'VE **EVER** BEEN!!

THAT DEFINITELY PROVES ONE THING....

....CELLULITE FLOATS..

SLUPPTTT

KNOW WHAT I WANNA GET, MOM?....A TATTOO.

ERK?

YOU KNOW, MAYBE A SNAKE OR A DRAGON ON MY CHEST. NOTHING BIG. — WITH CROSSED SWORDS, OR A FLAMING SPEAR?

OR, HOW'BOUT A HEART: JUST ABOUT HERE. — THE KIND WHERE YOU WRITE SOMEONE'S NAME UNDERNEATH?

I WAS ALSO THINKING ABOUT GETTING MY EAR PIERCED. I SAW A GUY WEARING A STUD WITH A CHAIN ON IT, AN'IT LOOKED PRETTY COOL.

WELL, UH, HONEY, THOSE ARE INTERESTING IDEAS; HOWEVER, ITS IMPORTANT FOR YOU TO CONSIDER THE SOCIAL IMPLICATIONS —AND THE FACT THAT THESE THINGS ARE PERMANENT IS.....

....AND, NATURALLY, WE WOULDN'T WANT TO DISCOURAGE YOU, BUT THERE COULD COME A DAY WHEN YOU'D REGRET HAVING.....

THE OLDER ONE GETS — THE MORE SOPHISTICATED THE ATTENTION-GETTING DEVICE!!

Our house in Dundas, Ontario, had a large front yard and several big shade trees that turned red, copper, and cartoon yellow every fall. Then, all that color would be dumped on our lawn.

The house that I draw in the strip is based on the Dundas house. It was on a pretty ravine in a pleasant suburb where neighbors cared and shared.

Every year, we all hoped that a strong wind would come along and blow all the leaves off our properties . . . onto the property next door. Wind or no wind, there were always great piles of leaves to rake, to bag, and to play in.

One of my most pleasant memories is watching our son, Aaron (who was then about four) climb into the raked leaves, pull them over him like a blanket, then lie down and go to sleep.

I should have taken photographs. Still, in my mind I can see that small, round face in the confetti of autumn and it pleases me so much to bring this memory "to life" again.

Drawings like this one are done for the "mother" in me!

75

I travel so often that I keep an overnight bag packed and ready to go. Every trip, it seems, involves a cab ride somewhere: to and from airports, to and from hotels. The drivers are always interesting—even the ones who don't talk. Most often, they are men from faraway places who have come to North America with little more than a map and a suitcase to start their lives over again for the sake and the safety of their children. Many have university degrees. Many are professionals, unable to obtain the documents that would allow them to continue their careers here. All of them have stories to tell: the kind of stories that novels and documentaries are made of, the kind of stories that defy your belief and understanding.

*   *   *

Our small plane landed in a blizzard. Ottawa's weather can be unpredictable in winter, and we were glad to have squeaked onto the runway just before the airport was closed! I was on my way to work on an animation project. The studio was about twenty minutes' drive from the flight base, and the driver who came for me could barely see through his windshield. It was one of those days when you wished you could have just stayed home.

A typical Canadian, I wedged myself into the backseat of his cab and grumbled about the weather. The conversation I've repeated here in this Sunday page happened just as you see it. Word for word. What I wrote was compelling . . . but it's only a portion of what he told me.

In the few minutes it took to drive to town, this soft-spoken, articulate, and courageous young man changed my attitude that day forever.

This page ran on January 3, 1993. Something to start off the new year. Something I thought I should share.

Man, you never know what you're going to find in your mailbox! After this strip ran, I received a package from a doctor in Des Moines, Iowa, containing—wait for it—a pair of video game gloves!! Yes, after treating a number of folks afflicted with painful video digititis (Nintendo knuckle), this compassionate and enterprising chap actually designed and manufactured a therapeutic device that both braces and supports those fiery phalanges, enabling the sufferer to pack in even more long hours at the blitz box!

Naturally, I was delighted to receive these trusses *de* tube, and wrote to thank him for his generosity.

This isn't the only neat invention I've had sent to me. Following a nocturnal comic strip scene in which Elly falls prey to the hazards of the "open bowl," I was presented with a device called the "Potty Light" that comes on automatically if the toilet seat is left up! It's a must in countless households, I'm sure.

I've received elastic "hugs," rubber bugs, T-shirts, family photos, diaries, dog hair, obituaries, psychic readings, children's drawings, cartoon folios, baby gifts, homemade cards . . . the kind of things one sends to a friend. When the reader mail comes, I do feel as though I'm hearing from friends.

Come to think of it, cartoonists' mailboxes are our link to the outside world. I mean, how else would my "support group" find me?

You never know what you're going to find in your mailbox.

Good thing we have a big one!

82

Why do they make bathing suits with those stupid egg-cups on them anyway? Is there a woman on earth they're designed to fit?

I consider myself to be average, OK? Average, average, average. By the time one's age-o-meter has clicked past forty, "average" is considered to be a plus. There are millions of us out there—and whenever we're not juggling careers, chaos, and the challenges of raising teenage children, what are we doing? We are trying to track down a garment manufacturer who sews for the body that is *@!*?!! **average**!!!

What's with the mastiff shoulders, gorilla-length arms, six-inch waists, and skirts designed to gird the loins of an undernourished twelve-year-old boy?!! And . . . what's with the bathing suits?

Summer fashions appear at the exact time we are trying to find clothing for spring. March is when the bathing suits arrive. March is when the average female begins the fruitless foray into the land of Lycra, hoping to find bathing togs that will (A) cover, (B) flatter, and (C) allow for some participation in water sports.

Hoping for two out of three, we search once more for a suit that's suitable. Hah! This is a project for the Discovery Channel!! Two years ago, I accidentally found a three-out-of-three!! Shocked and grateful, I ordered four of them (all the same) so I am set now for multiple seasons to come!! Alas . . .

This doesn't mean that I don't still (on a "thin day") try on those high-thigh, egg-cupped disasters with the hope that maybe I can look like the siliconed sylph in the window.

Why do we do it? Every year, we allow our self-esteem to be reduced to the size of bacteria. Every year we struggle in Port-a-John–sized cubicles, trying to get into and out of a garment that's guaranteed to disgust. And, every year we do this (heaven forbid) at the risk of exposure!

It's that old nightmare, isn't it? The average person's worst fear (aside from public speaking) is to be seen naked, or nearly naked, by someone other than one's spouse!

The fear of being seen in one of these egg-cupped creations was the catalyst for this Sunday strip. As a form of therapy, I guess, I had a hapless heroine streak through a shopping mall in "the bathing suit from hell."

After all . . . isn't it nice to see the things we fear most . . . happening to someone else?

Nearly every Thursday, my friend Beth brings her three children to my house to swim. Prior to the discovery that his body had buoyancy, her small son, Bourton, insisted on wearing a life jacket, inflatable arm rings, and an inner tube before he would enter the pool! This earned him the nickname "Mr. Floatation" and was the inspiration for this strip.

I look forward to these Thursday swims. I enjoy the noise and the action and the company. Since we both lead such busy lives, it's one of the few times I see Beth, and I like to have a conversation with her— if I can!

One day, as the kids demanded more and more of her attention, I said to her, "Beth, won't it be nice when they're grown up and you can have some spare time?" She looked at me with surprise and answered, "Lynn, this is my spare time!! Look at me: I'm playing in a swimming pool, I get to sit in the park and feed the squirrels, I get to walk with my stroller down Main Street. In a few years, I won't be doing these things—I'll be working! This," she said pointedly, "is my spare time!!"

It was a message that really hit home. How I wish I'd had Beth's perspective when Aaron and Kate were little.

Such comments are filed away in my mental Rolodex to await the time when I'll have both the courage and the honesty to use them!

Thirty was easy money. Thirty-five and forty went by like a breeze. I wondered about all those people so obsessed with their countenance that they'd seek corrective surgery and I gloated with satisfaction, knowing I wasn't going to be one of them. An aging visage was not a problem for me. That is until I turned forty-five.

Shortly after my forty-fifth birthday, I walked into the bathroom, looked in the mirror, and saw . . . somebody else. Aaaaugh!!!

Chin hairs? Bags? Neck wattles? Where did they come from—and why didn't they give me a chance to adjust? How could they appear overnight?

I saw a face that vaguely resembled the one I'd been washing for forty-five years . . . but, it was older. Much older. And, I wasn't ready for the blow.

Some folks deal with these earth-shattering truths by battling the inevitable. They diet, aerobicize, meditate, shed their seersucker for spandex . . . me? I draw cartoons. "Theratoons."

It's cartoons like this that make me the most vulnerable. It's cartoons like this that reveal the real "Me." It's also the sort of painful disclosure that elicits personal responses from readers (of all genders) reassuring me that I am not alone. "You want to see deterioration?" they say, "Check this!!" Yes, this job has saved my sanity.

It's thanks to this kind reassurance that I am now able to look into the mirror with objectivity, maturity, and acceptance. It's commiseration like this that enables me to . . . wait a minute . . .wait a minute . . . Was that wart there yesterday? Was that line so deep? Wait a minute, I'm not ready yet. Wait!

I said, I'm not ready!!!!!!

Lawrence's Story

In April 1993, I did a four-week story that really caused quite a stir! Because we have been asked by many readers what happened during that time, my editors and I thought it would be appropriate to include a follow-up to "Lawrence's Story" in this book.

Lawrence has been Michael Patterson's close friend and neighbor for many years. He has always been "the kid next door." For the longest time, he appeared consistently with Michael and his friends—but a few years ago, I began to find it harder and harder to bring Lawrence into the picture. Somehow, his life had taken a different turn and I couldn't quite understand why he wasn't still part of the gang. I began to concentrate on him, see his room, his things, his life.

I know all of these people so well. I know where their houses are, what their furniture's like, where they work. I know their voices and their mannerisms, their thoughts are open to me . . . and yet, I couldn't connect with Lawrence.

After "being" with him for some time, I realized that the reason he was having so much trouble communicating with Michael and his friends was because Lawrence, now in his late teens, was different. Lawrence was gay.

It felt right for Lawrence to be gay. He was like so many people I know who have had to deal with this traumatic realization and who have done so with courage and honesty.

For Better or For Worse has always been a sort of real-life chronicle, a look into the workings of a family and a neighborhood—an average neighborhood that could be in any town, anywhere.

Although I have focused on the lighter side, it has been important for me to explore those things in life that are not necessarily laughable, but, things that pose a challenge, things that must be dealt with seriously and worked through.

If the Pattersons were an average family in an average neighborhood, they would at some time be aware of the diversity in the people around them and would have to accept and try to understand those differences.

I felt that I was being true to life and to my work if I gave Lawrence the courage to tell Michael he was gay. I wanted to challenge myself, to see if I could broach a sensitive subject and write it into the strip with care and compassion. I included a bit of laughter, too.

Much thought went into this story. I must have had it in mind for two years or more before I wrote the series. I told my editor, Lee Salem, what I was planning to do. He suggested I send him my rough work, well in advance of the publication date, so that he could see what elements were involved and make deletions, if necessary. I wrote and sent in the material eight weeks before my deadline. Although Lee cautioned me that it was a sensitive issue and there could be some negative response, he felt that I had written the story well, that it contained no offensive material, and, that if I wished to run it, he and Universal Press would be supportive.

The four-week series was put into production and included with the "slicks" (the camera-ready art) was a letter to the editors from Lee, suggesting that they read the story before pasting up their comic pages. If they felt they would prefer to run alternate material, a set of previously run strips had been selected to fill that space.

Within a few days of receiving the package, forty newspapers declined the series and asked for the alternative strips. Many, however, for one reason or another never read the accompanying letter (or the strips) and were taken by complete surprise when the story appeared on their comic page and their phones began to ring!

Lee had warned me that there could be some concern—but none of us was prepared for the overwhelming event that followed.

As soon as the first panel ran, both the syndicate and the newspapers were swamped with phone calls. Some installed new systems just to handle the volume. Faxes and letters began to arrive, letters to editors, to Universal Press, to me. A spontaneous, emotional outpouring of opinion flooded into the system, and became, I think, one of the most impressive and intense reactions on record to a comic strip story. A young man admitted to his friend that he was gay and a Pandora's box was opened wide. All of us were shaken.

If I had shown one of the characters shooting another in a school yard, there would have been some reaction, I am certain, but it would have been nothing compared to the controversy started by this story. It totally floored us all.

At first, it seemed as though the response was mostly negative. Letters (that appeared to have been written in haste and rage) accused, threatened, cursed, and damned. Many, quoting elaborate passages from the Bible, included threatening and unprintable messages. "Curious thing," I thought to myself, "that these people felt they were worthy to sit in judgment of others." Some letters came as organized protests (many from people who, you could tell, had never read For Better or For Worse). Some came from people, who had been violated as children, equated homosexuality with pedophilia and thought I was in support of something that had destroyed their lives. The opposing points of view were varied, definite, and strong.

Within one week, nineteen papers had canceled For Better or For Worse outright. Editors who decided to run the series were attacked for having the gall to do so. Those who chose not to run it were accused of "censorship." Editors and publishers were damned if they did, and damned if they didn't. They called the syndicate. Editors at Universal Press worked overtime, diffusing the anger, answering questions, calming, and reassuring these people who were being harrassed, picketed, and were in the eye of a storm generated by ignorance. Those editors who wished to confront me personally were given my phone number. My phone rang constantly from 7 A.M. to 10 P.M. every day. I answered all my calls. I spoke with everyone who needed to know why, what was I trying to do? Did I realize what I had done?

Editors, particularly from smaller communities, were in the most uncomfortable position. In rural areas, where everybody knows everyone else, they were singled out, their children were harrassed at school. One editor confessed to me that his brother was gay. He was 100 percent supportive but if anyone in his area knew that he was in favor of running the story he would lose his job.

It was mostly from the United States that the sound was heard. Canadian papers carried the pro and con letters on the editorial pages. There were two cancellations and a few letters came to me, but by and large, it was a southern and very religious population that responded first and loudest and with a clenched, unyielding fist.

I cannot deny that it was upsetting. When 1,000 people organized to cancel their subscriptions to a Memphis paper, one editor's bitterness came through loud and clear. I had no right to "do this" to people. This subject was best left alone.

I think the letter that hurt most, was one of the first I received. It was from a woman who said she had loved my work for years but I was now no longer welcome in her home. She enclosed about a dozen yellowed strips she had kept on her refrigerator. That made me cry.

All of this, we called the "no" mail.

The people who decided to follow the story awhile, before voicing an opinion, began to respond a little later. By the time the second week of the story was under way, the positive side came forward. The phones and faxes continued to ring, but this time, the mail was an overwhelming positive, "Yes!"

The "Yes" mail came from doctors, teachers, mental health professionals, clergy, social workers, friends, and families of those about whom the story was written.

It took awhile for gay and lesbian readers to respond. It was as if they were waiting to see if I told the story as it really was—or was it another attempt by someone from the outside, patronizing and sensationalizing in order to gain publicity?

The letters that came from these men and women were direct, honest, and amazingly personal. I don't know when I have been so moved. It is not possible to imagine how painful it is to be persecuted and reviled because you are different. These letters were evidence of that.

As the mail arrived, my assistant and I sorted the letters into boxes marked "Yes," "No," and "Articles." (We had many, many newspaper clippings!). Altogether, over 2,500 personal letters were counted, and, of these responses, over 70 percent were positive.

All of these letters were answered. All of them were read with respect and interest.

I recently turned these "boxes of emotion" over to the sociology department of our local university, where they are proving to be an intimate and invaluable insight into this side of our human nature.

I learned a great deal when we ran the Lawrence story. I learned that the comics page is a powerful communicator. I learned that people read our work and care about what we say. We all look forward every day to that one page in the paper where the small truths lie, hoping for a laugh, or a little sarcasm, or a punchline that will ease the burden just a bit. I learned that our work is taken seriously, and despite the reduction in numbers and size, the comics matter a great deal. Those of us who produce these panels have a responsibility to ourselves, our syndicates, our publishers, and our audience to use this space with conscience and with care.

I believe I did that with this story.

I believe it made a difference.

My syndicate and many editors allowed me to take a risk . . . and, yes, without question, it was the right thing to do!

That's not How They Do It on TV!

A For Better or For Worse Collection 1993-94
by Lynn Johnston

112

116

117

123

I DUNNO IF SHE'S GOING WITH ANYONE, MAN. - I STARTED WORKING HERE WHEN YOU DID!

WHY DON'T YOU ASK IF YOU CAN DRIVE HER HOME, MIKE.

YEAH! - IF SHE SAYS "YES," YOU'RE GOLDEN!

IT'S ALMOST CLOSING TIME... I'M GONNA DO IT! I'M GONNA ASK THE GIRL AT CHECKOUT SIX IF I CAN DRIVE HER HOME. I'LL JUST GO UP TO HER AN'SAY...

RHETTA? PICK YOU UP AT THE FRONT DOOR... I'M IN THE BUS ZONE!!

NATURALLY. - I SHOULD HAVE KNOWN. RHETTA HAD A BOYFRIEND. IT FIGURES.

I ALMOST ASKED IF I COULD DRIVE HER HOME! - RIGHT IN FRONT OF HIM! HOW COULD I HAVE BEEN SO DUMB?

SHE THINKS I'M A DOOR-KNOB. I KNOW IT. SHE THINKS I'M A MEGANERD. ... A TWINKIE WITH A BOW TIE! AAAAUGH!

I THINK HE LIKES ME, LORNE!

COME ON, SIS. - YOU DON'T WANNA DATE A DWEEB FROM WORK!!

ONE OF THOSE NIGHTS, HUH. I MEAN, WHENEVER YOU WRITE IN YOUR DIARY, I KNOW SOMETHING HAPPENED.

SIGH

LOOKING AT ME, LIZ - HOW WOULD YOU DESCRIBE ME? YOU KNOW ... FROM A WOMAN'S POINT OF VIEW?

I'D CALL YOU A "HUNK"!

A HUNK? - REALLY?

WAIT A MINUTE! ... OF WHAT ?!

129

130

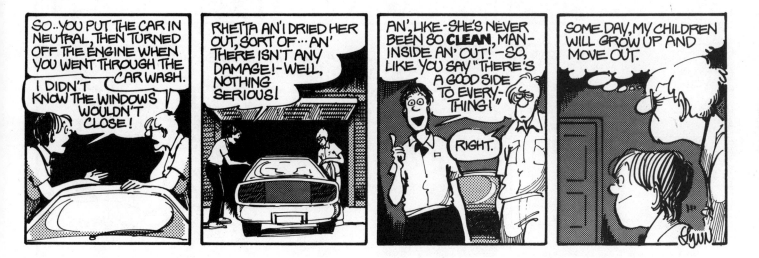

133

136

138

ISN'T IT GOOD TO HEAR THE PATTER OF TINY FEET ONCE AGAIN.

PRINCIPAL

HI, MISS EDWARDS!—HAVE A GOOD SUMMER?

SURE DID!

I WENT CAMPING WITH SOME FRIENDS, WE DID SOME CANOEING, SOME HIKING, SOME FISHING—AND SAW A LOT OF THE EAST COAST!

YOU DID ALL THOSE THINGS?

OF COURSE!

WHERE THERE'S A WHEEL, ...THERE'S A WAY!!

THEY PAINTED THE MAIN HALL!

YEAH!

...AN' THEY RE-ARRANGED THE TROPHY CASE.

THE CAFETERIA LOOKS THE SAME.

SO DOES THE SCIENCE LAB!

I CAN'T WAIT TO SEE EVERY-BODY!

ME TOO.

IT'S NEAT, COMING BACK TO SCHOOL AFTER THE SUMMER HOLIDAYS!

YEAH.

.... IT'S LIKE COMING HOME.

146

147

150

151

AMAZING. I CAN'T BELIEVE YOU ACTUALLY STOPPED RUSH HOUR TRAFFIC, AND SHOUTED SLOGANS AT POLICE!

DAD, IT WAS A PROTEST!

AGAINST WHAT—THE 30% BUS FARE HIKE?—IT'S A 10% RAISE EVERY YEAR FOR 3 YEARS! THE CITY VOTED IN FAVOR OF IT LAST SPRING!

REALLY?

AND THE NEW FARES MEAN YOU CAN TRAVEL TWICE AS FAR!

...I NEVER KNEW THAT.

IGNORANCE ISN'T BLISS, MIKE.... IT'S DANGEROUS!!

WHY DID I **DO** IT? WHY, WHY, WHY, WHY, **WHY**?

I MADE A COMPLETE FOOL OF MYSELF!!—I WISH I HADN'T DONE IT! I WISH, I WISH, I WISH, I WISH!!

IF I COULD GO BACK TO THIS MORNING....IF I COULD CHANGE JUST THIS **ONE** DAY!!

⸮SIGH⸮....WHOEVER INVENTS A TIME MACHINE WILL MAKE A ZILLION BUCKS!!

HI.

DAD.....I AM SO EMBARRASSED. WHY DID I JOIN A PROTEST RALLY—WHEN I DIDN'T EVEN KNOW WHAT WAS GOING ON?

WESLEY SAID IT WAS RIGHT, AN' I BELIEVED HIM. WE ALL FOLLOWED HIM WITHOUT QUESTION. ...WE WERE WRONG.

WHAT A DUMB THING TO DO. I WISH TODAY HAD NEVER HAPPENED.

I DON'T.

WHY?

...BECAUSE YOU LEARNED FROM IT.

158

SNORKKK

SCRATCH...

MICHAEL, WHY DO YOU LOOK SO SLOPPY? - IS IT SOME KIND OF "SPECIAL DAY" TODAY?

GRUNCH

YOU MIGHT SAY THAT.....

- THEY'RE TAKING SCHOOL PHOTOGRAPHS.

WHAT?!! - YOU'RE NOT SERIOUS!

THAT'S THE WAY IT IS.

NEXT!

WHY DIDN'T THEY TELL US THE SCHOOL PHOTOGRAPHER WAS ONLY TAKING ONE POSE?

COUPLE'A GUYS ARE GOIN' OVER TO BRIAN'S TONIGHT. - ARE YOU COMING, MIKE?

NAH. I GOTTA WORK.

WORK! - COME ON, MAN. BETWEEN THAT AN' HOMEWORK, YOU DON'T GET ANY TIME OFF!

I WANNA BUY A CAR, GORD.

I WANT MY OWN WHEELS!

HOO.. THAT MEANS GAS AN' INSURANCE, AN' PAYMENTS AN' REPAIRS ...YOU'RE GONNA BE SO TIED UP IN BILLS - YOU WON'T KNOW WHAT HIT YOU!!

WELL... THAT'S THE PRICE OF FREEDOM!

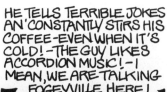

168

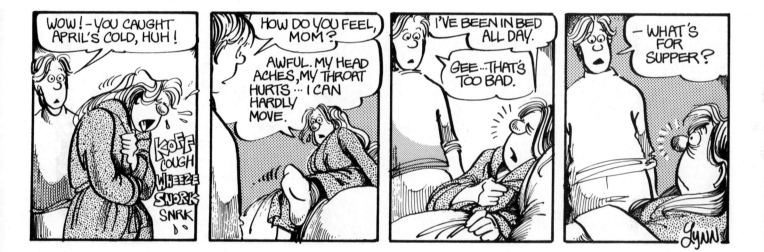

171

174

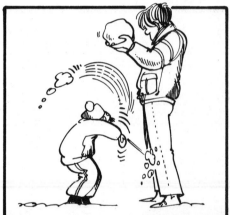

BOOF!

WHAT'S GOING ON OUTSIDE?

MIKE AN' APRIL ARE HAVING A SNOWBALL FIGHT!

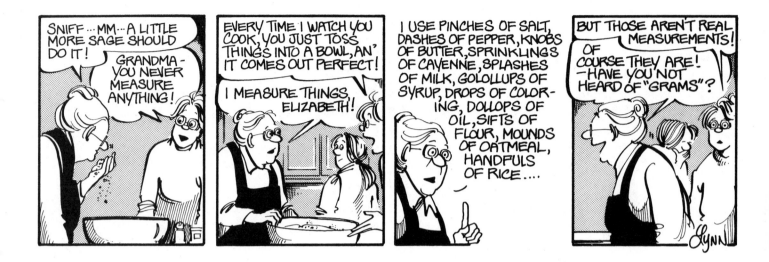

181

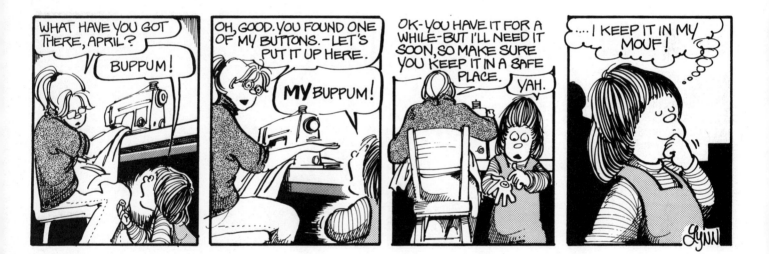

187

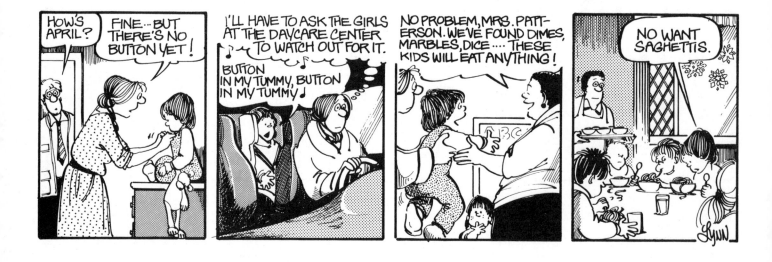

190

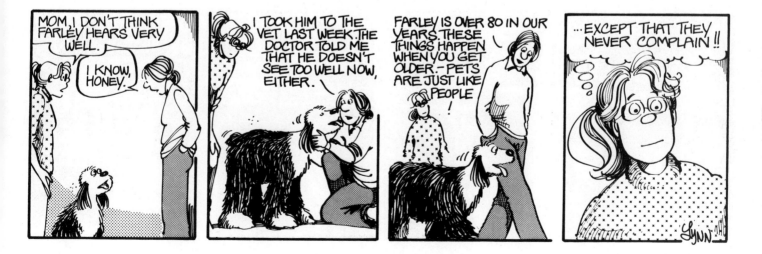

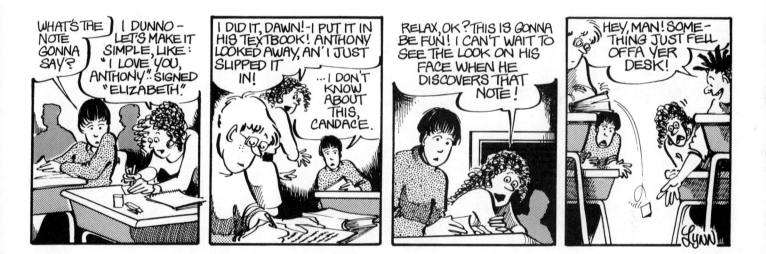

195

199

200

201

203

TSK! - THERE'S A MOUSE IN THE KITCHEN. HE'S CHEWED ON THE GARBAGE, AND HE'S LEFT HIS CALLING CARDS.

I HATE TO TRAP THEM, BUT THEY MAKE SUCH A MESS!!

YEAH. TOO BAD.

IF ANIMALS SURVIVE BY ADAPTING TO THEIR ENVIRONMENT, WHY HASN'T EVOLUTION CREATED A MESSLESS MOUSE?

CHEESE

... EVOLUTION IS STILL WORKING ON THE HIGHER LIFE FORMS.

OATY UFFS

MILK

Lynn

SNIFF, SNORK, SNUFF, SNUFF

BANG!

WHAK!

... MUST HAVE BEEN A BIG MOUSE! ... AND HE GOT AWAY.

Lynn

DARN. THIS TRAP HAS BEEN SPRUNG AGAIN .... - AND NO MOUSE!!

I DON'T WANT YOU TO TRAP HIM, MOM - THEY'RE SO CUTE!

ELIZABETH, JUST BECAUSE SOMETHING'S CUTE DOESN'T MEAN IT HAS THE RIGHT TO MESS UP MY KITCHEN!

Lynn

204

206

211

212

For Better or For Worse
By Lynn Johnston

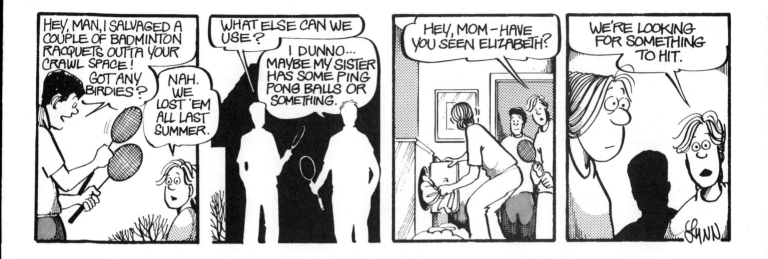

224

226

227